Evaluating community projects

NIACE lifelines in adult learning

The *NIACE lifelines in adult learning* series provides straightforward background and information, accessible know-how and useful examples of good practice for all practitioners involved in adult and community learning. Focusing in turn on different areas of adult learning these guides are an essential part of every practitioner's toolkit.

1. **Community education and neighbourhood renewal** – Jane Thompson, ISBN 1 86201 139 7
2. **Spreading the word: reaching out to new learners** – Veronica McGivney, ISBN 1 86201 140 0
3. **Managing community projects for change** – Jan Eldred, ISBN 1 86201 141 9
4. **Engaging black learners in adult and community education** – Lenford White, ISBN 1 86201 142 7
5. **Consulting adults** – Chris Jude, ISBN 1 86201 194 4
6. **Working with young adults** – Carol Jackson, ISBN 1 86201 150 8
7. **Promoting learning** – Kate Malone, ISBN 1 86201 151 6
8. **Evaluating community projects** – Jane Field, ISBN 1 86201 152 4
9. **Working in partnership** – Lyn Tett, ISBN 1 86201 162 1

Forthcoming titles
10. **Working with Asian heritage communities** – David McNulty, ISBN 1 86201 174 5
11. **Learning and community arts** – Jane Thompson, ISBN 1 86201 181 8
12. **Museums and community learning** – Garrick Fincham, ISBN 1 86201 182 6
13. **Libraries and community learning** – John Pateman, ISBN 1 86201 183 4

Evaluating community projects

Jane Field

Published by the National Institute of
Adult Continuing Education (England and Wales)

21 De Montfort Street
Leicester LE1 7GE
Company registration no. 2603322
Charity registration no. 1002775

First published 2003

© 2003 National Institute of Adult Continuing Education (England and Wales)

All rights reserved. No reproduction, copy or transmission of this publication may be made without the written permission of the publishers, save in accordance with the provisions of the Copyright, Designs and Patents Act 1988, or under the terms of any licence permitting limited copying issue by the Copyright Licensing Agency.

The *NIACE lifelines in adult learning series* is supported by the Adult and Community Learning Fund. ACLF is funded by the Department for Education and Skills and managed in partnership by NIACE and the Basic Skills Agency to develop widening participation in adult learning.

niace
promoting adult learning

NIACE has a broad remit to promote lifelong learning opportunities for adults. NIACE works to develop increased participation in education and training, particularly for those who do not have easy access because of barriers of class, gender, age, race, language and culture, learning difficulties and disabilities, or insufficient financial resources.

www.niace.org.uk

Cataloguing in Publication Data
A CIP record of this title is available from the British Library

All photographs courtesy of Richard Olivier unless otherwise stated
Designed and typeset by Boldface
Printed in Great Britain by Russell Press, Nottingham

ISBN 1 86201 152 4

Acknowledgements

I would like to dedicate this book to my children – Tom, Jesse and Annie – and to friends, family and work colleagues who have given support in many ways, and encouragement to try out new ideas. I am particularly pleased that the 'inspirations' demonstrate some of the outstanding community development that is happening in Belfast today.

Contents

1	Why does evaluation matter?	1
2	Key concepts	3
3	Getting started and how to go about it	6
4	Internal monitoring	8
5	External monitoring	13
6	Evaluation approaches and tools	17
7	Making a difference	21
8	Qualitative indicators	25
9	Building in sustainability	28
10	Spreading the word	31
11	Check it out	32
	Glossary	33
	Further reading, resources and websites	34

Note to the reader
Inspirations: refer to case studies and examples of good practice.
Glossary: the meanings of the words underlined in the text can be found in the glossary on page 33.

1 Why does evaluation matter?

Anyone involved in running a community-based project will be used to (and may dread) hearing the following questions:

"How can you show that this project is worth continuing?"

"What has the project done for the people living in this community?"

"Why should we continue to fund your project?"

Effective project evaluation will provide many of the answers to these questions. Building evaluation structures and processes into the project from the first day is one way to ensure that any project can 'capture' data that can be used to show what has been achieved, how this has happened, and the impact of the project with the target group and further afield. The data that is recorded should be both quantitative and qualitative. It should include feedback taken from the project team, people in the community, beneficiaries, stakeholders, statutory agencies, the voluntary sector and others that have been involved with the project.

The evaluation process can record:

- the number of people involved in various elements of the project such as learners, children attending crèche facilities, participants at project events;
- the work of the project team – courses delivered, home visits, fun days;
- views of project participants – looking at what they learnt or enjoyed about a course, how the project has helped them individually, within the family, in the community to gain employment;
- views of agencies to whom the project is complementary eg. Health Trusts, education institutions, Learning and Skills Councils;
- good practice – what has worked well;
- constraints – areas where the project has faced obstacles or barriers;
- problems encountered and solutions found;
- impact – how the project has made a difference;
- benefits to individuals, groups and communities.

Furthermore, evaluation provides accountability; to the project team, the project management committee, the community and funding bodies. Community development projects are largely funded through public expenditure of one sort or another. The evaluation process helps to show how the project money has been spent. It can show inputs and outputs (efficiency measures), value for money and cost-effectiveness. However, community development projects are concerned about more than this; they are about empowering individuals and regenerating communities. Many projects also want to encourage individuals and communities to think and work more proactively in terms of their own development. These issues are less tangible than simply recording and analysing numerical data; but for community development projects are highly significant, and should not be relegated to a minor element of the evaluation process.

To evaluate means "to ascertain or set the amount or value of; to judge or assess the worth of; to appraise" (*Collins English Dictionary*). The evaluation process should relate to the needs and objectives of the organisation, project staff, the management committee, the beneficiaries, the stakeholders and the funding organisation. It should be a coherent process that starts with expectations, leads through to reaction and measures the changes. The evaluation process should be appropriate to the activity being evaluated and needs to include effective feedback systems to all those involved; which may then contribute to project review and future development.

In simple terms, evaluation is about asking the question 'how do you know what you think you know, and where is the evidence?'. It involves adopting a methodology and a framework within which the project can be evaluated. Evaluation can be undertaken internally, by an external evaluator or by the funding body. This Lifeline focuses on internal evaluation processes and the potential role of an external evaluator appointed by the project.

The Bridge, East Belfast

"We need to think about what the evaluation is there to do. We need clear outcomes and the project should be monitored throughout. This helps us to keep up to date with what is happening."

2 Key concepts

Evaluation may either be formative or summative; or use both approaches. Summative evaluation happens towards the end of the project. The disadvantage of solely using a summative approach is that it may take place at a time when project staff are looking for other jobs, and funding is not immediately (if ever) available to implement evaluation findings. The summative evaluation report may be seen more as a historical document, rather than a tool that can be used to inform project review and development.

Effective evaluation should contribute to the learning process and the development of a project rather than simply ticking boxes and informing project management about where the project has 'passed' or 'failed'. Through the use of a number of evaluation processes the evaluator has the benefit of inside knowledge about all aspects of the work of the project, without being 'bogged down' by the day-to-day operations. Thus it is possible to encourage key players and participants to reflect on what is happening; thereby identifying good practice, enabling strategies and areas of constraint or conflict. Formative evaluation contributes to the learning process not only to the benefit of the project and the partners but also for the benefit of the project funders. In short, the external evaluator might be seen as a 'critical friend'.

The evaluation process should consider the impact of a project; for the project team, stakeholders, partners and beneficiaries. The evaluator can observe and seek opinions on the extent to which objectives and outcomes initially agreed are met during the lifetime of the project. The evaluation can also look at the added value gained from participation in the project; this may be from the viewpoint of communities, stakeholder organisations, beneficiaries and/or individuals.

The evaluation process can support the project, not only in terms of general development, but also through the delivery of reports that can be included when formally reporting on the project to the funding body. Furthermore, experience shows that in many cases evaluation activities add to project staff's motivation, providing an opportunity to reflect on what has been done, recognise achievements, discuss both short-term and longer-term priorities and 'brainstorm' future challenges.

At the same time it is important to keep evaluation in perspective. Project beneficiaries should not be made to feel like guinea-pigs, under constant scrutiny and subject to endless questionnaires and interviews. At the UACE Conference in

1993 Bill Williamson, when talking about quality controls, said, "There is a real danger that quality controls quickly degenerate into controls, and controls too easily stifle creativity, imagination and risk-taking – all of which are at the core of educational experiences of a challenging and enriching kind". The same analogy can be made of evaluation; evaluation can be used to support development and risk taking. Sometimes more can be learnt by looking at what went wrong, and there is a need to celebrate failure and learn for the future. Projects provide an opportunity to take risks and to try new things. The evaluation can help a project see what is working, why it is working and what impact this is having on the individual, the community and potentially on more mainstream service delivery. It should not get in the way of project development, implementation and innovation, but rather contribute to the learning and review process. Furthermore, the evaluation should take into account what is happening at a wider level, ie. what influence (if any) are external events making to the project; as well as the impact of the project both for individuals and communities.

INSPIRATIONS

The OASIS Centre
IMAGO Project – befriending those with mental ill-health difficulties

"We employed the evaluator from the start of the project. She has provided seven interim evaluation reports in the first 18 months of the project, including benefits to IMAGO clients and the befrienders (who were all previously unemployed), case stories, feedback from the referrers (all health professionals) and an end-of-year report. We have found that she has an overview of what we are setting out to achieve, asks a lot of questions – sometimes difficult ones that we didn't necessarily want to hear but made us think, suggests alternative ideas and keeps us on track through the experience she had gleaned from other projects that she had been involved with. We have confidence in our evaluator and know what is being done and why it is being done."

The Bridge, East Belfast

"Evaluation is a waste of time if it is not a living document."

University of Plymouth: Advice and Guidance for Students with Disabilities

"Ongoing formative evaluation directly contributed to the learning and development process of the project. At the very beginning the questionnaire to the steering group (issued following a group evaluation exercise) asked everyone to identify what they saw as the priorities for the project. We realised that some of the phrases used within the university (for example 'student led') were not understood by external members of the steering group; which encouraged us to better communicate concepts. Good practice and constraints were evaluated on a regular basis and it was interesting that we forgot things implemented at the start of the project as they were taken as second nature (for example, producing materials for dyslexic students on cream paper, in blue ink using 14-point Arial font). Without the evaluation we might have lost sight of some of the areas in which the project was successful and made a lasting difference to practice."

3 Getting started and how to go about it

It is a good idea to include evaluation in the initial project proposal budget; which will provide the financial resources to undertake the evaluation. Interestingly some funding bodies still question the need for evaluation, often saying that they will evaluate the project themselves. However, this is usually at the end (ie. summative) and may not include all the areas of evaluation that are of interest to the project team and stakeholders. Furthermore such an evaluation may not happen in time to support the project development, learning process, and review. It is useful to outline the role of the evaluation within the project proposal; showing how evaluation will benefit the project.

Internal monitoring systems need to be established from the start; this is discussed further in the next section.

If the decision is made to appoint an external evaluator the standard process is to draw up an evaluation tender. This will usually include:

- project aims, objectives and outcomes;
- a brief background to the project;
- the aims and objectives of the evaluation;
- the time scale for the evaluation;
- request for specific information from the evaluation team;
- evaluation approach and methodology;
- relevant expertise and/or brief CV of all staff;
- previous experience of the evaluation team;
- number of days, and cost per day for each member of the evaluation team;
- evaluation milestones;
- deliverables.

It is also worth considering that there are benefits in keeping the evaluation process relatively flexible. This will allow for specific issues to be evaluated, which may not have been originally anticipated. For example, the project may develop in a way that was not initially anticipated which, if particularly innovative, may benefit from evaluation. Alternatively, the evaluation may be used to help the project address a particular problem.

Having put the evaluation out to tender it may be appropriate to invite some of the applicants in to discuss the evaluation process, most usually with the project coordinator and some members of the project management committee. This allows for useful discussion about the evaluation process, how it will happen, and what will be done, as well as seeing whether the person will work well with the project team, and has a good understanding about issues pertinent to the particular project to be evaluated.

East Belfast Community Development Agency

"Sometimes pilot projects get caught up with the 'bums on seats' mentality; this is not about impact. And at other times the funders want you to reduce or take out the evaluation costs, but if they do, it is just a number crunching exercise that doesn't take into account what has happened in the community as a result of the project. We need to make sure that we can have our projects evaluated by someone who has an understanding of what community development is about."

4 Internal monitoring

Projects may choose to undertake some or all of the evaluation themselves. All projects will need to develop systems to undertake basic internal monitoring to record the work that is being done on a day-to-day basis. This will include recording:

- quantifiable targets;
- time-based targets;
- how project objectives are being met;
- resources and value for money.

Developing internal monitoring systems should be included as one of the initial priorities for any project, as retrospective recording is time consuming and more difficult to do.

Recording quantifiable targets should be the responsibility of the individual member of staff involved in delivering the project. Quantitative targets may include:

- community events organised;
- participants involved in different activities, such as courses, home visits, crèches, open days;
- dissemination activities such as presentations, written papers, seminars;
- completed surveys and questionnaires;
- networking, for example, visits, meetings, conferences.

Recording quantitative targets is most easily done through devising a series of internal monitoring forms, completed on a weekly or monthly basis. Experience shows that often project staff do not see this paperwork as essential; in practice it is imperative that work is recorded on a regular basis, and that the collation of internal monitoring forms is circulated among the management team. Funding organisations will also usually require records of quantitative targets, which may have been identified in the funding proposal.

Time-based targets will be of greater concern to the project manager, who will need to know whether tasks were completed on time and to the standard required. It is also useful to keep a record of whether deadlines were effectively met.

Meeting deadlines may impinge on other elements of the project being effectively actioned. At times consultation about realistic deadlines may result in better time management across the project, particularly if contributions made during discussion are respected.

It is a valuable exercise to record how project objectives are being met through project development and delivery. Project staff should be encouraged to think about the original objectives and how the delivery of the project is meeting these objectives. Internal monitoring can address:

- to what extent was each project's objective achieved?
- what is the outcome of achieving the objectives?
- if problems occurred, what mechanisms and strategies were employed to continue the momentum of the project?

This may be done through discussion at team meetings. External evaluators will also want to address issues around project objectives and can support this process. One way of keeping the project objectives in mind is to encourage all project workers to consider which objectives are being contributed to (either significantly or in part) when drawing up action plans or completing internal monitoring forms.

The project manager will need to monitor the project budget. Many projects establish a finance sub-group, drawing on the expertise of members of the management committee. Issues for ongoing monitoring include:

- is the original budget allocation appropriate to need?
- regular budget review and revision if appropriate?
- have any additional resources been generated?
- in what ways has the project demonstrated value for money?

Projects can experience a number of problems when developing internal monitoring systems. It is worthwhile to be aware of where problems can lie; they include:

- defining objectives;
- agreeing roles;
- setting targets;
- planning the evaluation strategy;
- collecting baseline data;
- agreeing reporting procedures;
- formative vs summative evaluation.

There may be some resistance and reluctance from project workers to complete internal monitoring forms. It is often seen as less of a priority than real time project development and implementation. However, effective project management includes maintaining comprehensive records, and the rationale and benefits need to be clearly explained to all staff and volunteers involved.

Engage With Age – Project Monitoring Form

Name:

Activity:

Venue:

Target Group:

Target Group	Male	Female	Total
50 – 65 years			
66 – 80 years			
Over 80 years			
Inter-generational (ie. all ages)			

Positive Feedback – eg. what participants enjoyed, what they learnt, things they might do differently as a result:

Negative feedback – eg. anything participants did not enjoy:

Lessons learnt for future activities – ie. how you might organise events differently, ideas for new activities, alternative venues:

Additional comments or thoughts:

Meeting Project Objectives:

Towards which of the Project objective/s do you think this activity/event has contributed?

Project Objective	Significant contribution	Some contribution
Strengthening community infrastructure affecting older people through the provision of training/capacity building		

Strengthening community infrastructure affecting older people through the development of older people's forums		
Strengthening community infrastructure affecting older people through expansion of activities and personal development		
Strengthening community infrastructure affecting older people through developing the ambassador programme		
Promoting inter/cross generational contact, understanding and relationships		
Developing networks and greater cohesion between providers of services to older people in the community		
Encouraging and supporting the implementation of interagency initiatives targeting the most isolated individuals in areas of high levels of deprivation		
Building meaningful interagency involvement and cooperation		
Raising awareness of Engage With Age among target beneficiaries		
Raising awareness of Engage With Age among partnership agencies		
Raising awareness of Engage With Age among funders		
Raising awareness of Engage With Age among policy makers		
Developing targeted initiatives/programmes for minority communities of older people		

Inner East Belfast Sure Start Project

It was agreed with the external evaluator that internal monitoring forms were needed for the following purposes:

Project area	Nature of the form	Rationale
Reception and office	To record incoming telephone calls and the nature of the enquiries	Identify type of calls to see the extent to which families and community groups are phoning the office; and other the nature of the other incoming calls
Reception and office	Telephone follow-up record in response to new parent enquiries	To ensure new parent enquiries are responded to promptly
Childcare workers	Weekly data sheet	To record the location of crèches, and the number and ages of children attending on a weekly basis

Childcare workers and parents	Child achievement certificate	To provide feedback on work done with the Sure Start children, to provide a check on areas covered for each course and a record for the parents, providing opportunities to discuss their child's development
Sure Start parents	Evaluation questionnaire	"Reactionnaire" to gain feedback from parents about the crèche facilities, record any changes in their child and any suggestions for improvement at the crèche
Health development workers	Weekly activity sheet	To record activities undertaken during each week, showing type of activity and location or organisation
Health development workers family proforma	Family proforma	Providing an update on the work with each individual family, showing issues discussed, action and any outcome or impact. Also a useful reminder prior to family visits.
Community Managers	Weekly data sheet	Record of number of children attending crèches and the number of weekly sessions; providing information about how the Sure Start childcare workers are deployed
Community Managers	Courses and crèches: monthly feedback form	Showing the types of courses and numbers attending; where Sure Start childcare workers are running crèches. This provides information about what training parents are interested in
Community Managers	Monthly feedback form	Data on training attended by Sure Start childcare workers. Also information about the impact of the Sure Start Project

5 External evaluation

Having decided to appoint an external evaluator it is important to understand what their role will be. In addition to specific evaluation activities agreed in the tender the external evaluator will be looking at:

- how the project was successful/not so successful?
- is it worth continuing or imitating elsewhere?
- what is the impact of the project?
- are there lessons and experience that can be transferred to future projects?
- where next, ie. what will happen when this project funding finishes?

The stages in the evaluation process will include:

- documentation review;
- accessing and collecting basic data;
- interviews and observation;
- analysis;
- reports;
- presentations;
- review.

The section below looks at different evaluation tools that may be used in some detail.

Issues that may be evaluated include:

- the project partnership;
- project aims and objectives (ie. the process of project implementation and delivery and the extent to which aims and objectives have been met);
- project outcomes, quantitative targets and outputs;
- products, resources or materials developed (as appropriate);
- specific project activities or elements;
- the project process;
- internal records;
- dissemination activities.

The external evaluation team can provide:

Interim evaluation reports: most project teams find benefit in receiving interim reports during the lifetime of the project. Depending on the approach, this may be the delivery of interim reports at agreed intervals, or may be a series of short reports on a number of specific issues throughout the project.

The final evaluation report: this will address the extent to which the project aims, objectives, targets and outcomes (as initially stated or revised) have been met; and will identify key issues, methods of delivery, innovation, good practice, enabling strategies and constraints. The content and format of the final evaluation report will be agreed between the project and the evaluation team. It may also meet specific guidelines specified by the funding body.

Insight into the impact of the Project: using a range of evaluation processes and tools (see below) the evaluator will observe and seek opinions to identify the impact of the project at both tangible and less tangible levels.

A contribution to the learning process: through reports and presentations external evaluation can support the learning and development process. Formal and informal discussion and review ensure that maximum benefit is gained from the external evaluation – without making time to discuss evaluation outcomes it may be that reports are only skim-read and the contents not fully utilised. One way of addressing this is to schedule presentations from the evaluator to project management committees or Boards, and to include a slot for the evaluator in other presentations, for example, to project funding bodies, statutory agencies and politicians.

INSPIRATIONS

Inner City South Belfast Sure Start Project

"One aspect of the evaluation focused on the relationship between Sure Start and the Health Visitors, who make referrals to the Project. First of all the evaluator used a postal questionnaire, but the feedback was very poor. She then spent two hours with the Health Visitors during a team meeting; and whilst getting a lot of positive feedback about the complementary nature of the project, the issue of lack of feedback from referrals came across very strongly. As a result we have built in two new systems, such that the Health Visitors have feedback about the state of play with the referral within 10 days and then a second form is sent once a Key Worker has started working with the family to feedback on the focus of this work. Not only has this shown that we respond to the findings of the evaluation, but also if this hadn't been identified in the formative evaluation process, then we may not have picked up on the issues, which would have been detrimental to the project in the longer term."

Inner East Belfast Sure Start Project

"It is important that the evaluation process can be flexible; sometimes external events happen that can have a major impact on the project. Our Sure Start Project used the external evaluator to carry out a piece of work that recorded and measured how the interface problems over the summer had an impact on both the project delivery and on staff relations. This not only provided a record of how the project targets were affected by the conflict; but also contributed to the Management Board review of how best to address staff issues that happened as a direct result of the troubles."

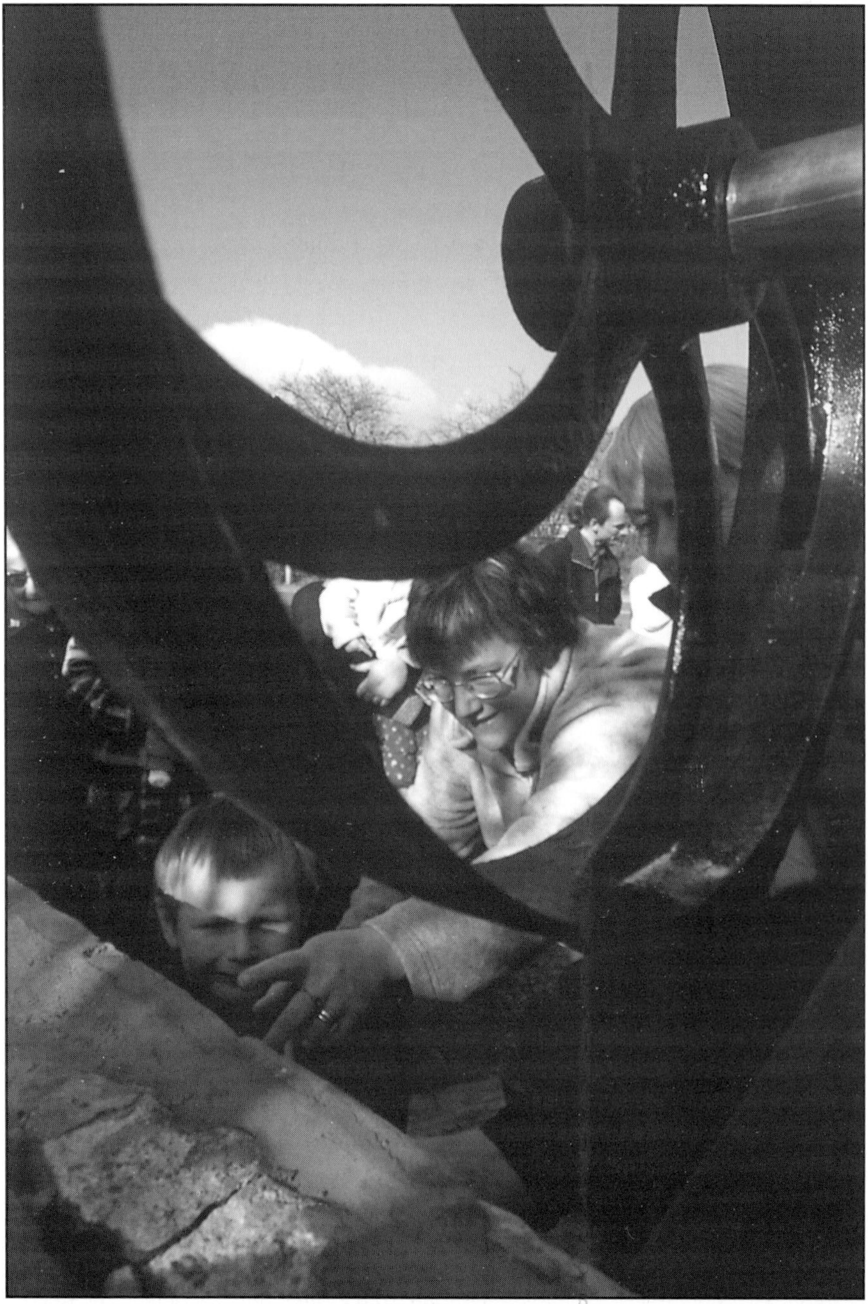

6 Evaluation approaches and tools

The evaluation process will embrace the use of a number of different evaluation tools in order to gain a comprehensive range of quantitative and qualitative data. These include:

- data collection;
- documentation review;
- support with the development of internal monitoring frameworks;
- questionnaires;
- telephone interviews;
- group discussion;
- story-telling and case stories;
- logbooks;
- focus groups;
- individual face-to-face interviews;
- attending meetings/observation;
- presentations.

Data collection
The evaluation team should collect quantitative data, often making use of internal monitoring data. Such data might include the number of participants, events, courses, visits and enquiries.

Documentation review
The evaluation team should have access to relevant project documentation, including minutes of meetings, new local and regional reports, and internal reports. This will enable the evaluators to keep abreast of the development and implementation of the project and how it relates to other policy and strategy developments. In addition, relevant theoretical material and published papers can also be reviewed and incorporated into discussion.

Support with the development of internal monitoring frameworks
The evaluation team may support the project team in the design and development of internal monitoring frameworks. The data gathered can then be used as an operational tool within the project team and contribute to the quantitative evaluation data.

Questionnaires

Postal questionnaires allow both quantitative and qualitative data of a similar nature to be collected, thereby gaining a picture of how different people perceive the development and delivery of the project, identifying good practice and constraints and leading to recommendations and setting priorities for the future. Questionnaires can be used with project staff, volunteers, members of management committees, participants, partners, and other stakeholders. As with the development of any questionnaire, the person designing the questionnaire should ensure that the questionnaire is well designed, think about what information they want to gain from the questions asked and consider methods of gaining maximum response. Interviews or focus groups may be used as a follow-up to questionnaires; to gain additional information and to look at specific issues in more depth.

Telephone interviews

Telephone interviews are usually more cost-effective than face-to-face interviews. Experience shows that they generate significant information; almost everyone is comfortable using the telephone, and people can feel more secure being in their own environment. Telephone interviews often elicit very open and honest feedback; for some it is easier to be constructively critical when not looking someone in the eye.

Individual face-to-face interviews

Interviews may be arranged between the evaluation team, and project staff, volunteers, partners, management committee members, beneficiaries, key players in the communities or other stakeholders. These interviews can focus on any number of issues, which may include recording the project process and implementation, good practice, constraints, challenges, or focusing on one particular topic or element of the project. They allow interviewees time to reflect and to consider future activity. Interviews also provide the opportunity for the evaluator to visit locations at which the project is being delivered, providing additional insight and understanding.

Group discussions

Group discussions can focus on specific issues, maybe in response to the need to address potential problems or challenges, or to look at particular activities. Approaches such as the SWOT analysis (strengths, weaknesses, opportunities and threats), GOAL (goals, objectives, achievements, and lessons learnt), brainstorming challenges, revisiting aims and objectives, and priority setting may be used in group discussions. These may be with the management boards, staff, representatives from community groups, beneficiaries, participants or any other significant group of people.

Story-telling and case stories
Recent experience shows that short anecdotes or stories can paint a picture of a project in action; which can then be used to demonstrate in practice what the project is doing. The aim of the stories is that they are 'brief-but-vivid' and relate elements of the project. The stories are told during group or one-to-one sessions with staff or beneficiaries demonstrating the impact of the project. When written, the stories are often anonymous.

Logbooks
Logbooks (diaries) can be used by staff or beneficiaries to record activities, what has been learnt, feelings or what individuals would like to do as a result of a project experience. They can be used over a short period, eg. every day for a week, which can be particularly useful over a time-bound activity such as a residential (when both staff and participants should be expected to complete the log); or once a week over an agreed period of time. Logbooks are most effective when a simple framework for recording is given for each entry.

Focus groups
Focus groups provide staff, beneficiaries, community representatives and others with the opportunity to reflect, for example on the impact of the project, changes that have taken place, or individual/community empowerment. Discussion can also to look at what might be done to further raise develop the project in the short- and longer-term future. Focus groups work well when those participating 'spark' ideas among themselves during discussion.

Attending meetings/observation
When appropriate the evaluator will attend management committee, project board and staff meetings. This will predominantly be to observe, but may also involve participation through presentations or facilitation.

Presentations
Presentations on the findings of the evaluation activity will ensure that staff, the management committee, board members and other stakeholders address issues identified during the evaluation process.

Through the use of a range of evaluation tools and processes – collecting both quantitative and qualitative data – the evaluator, and subsequently project stakeholders, will gain an understanding of the project; highlighting both areas in which the project is doing well, and areas for improvement.

INSPIRATIONS

Community Development Unit, South and East Belfast Trust

"We need to look at what will make people sit up and listen; different approaches work with different people. Our Chief Executive always wants to know how a project has made a difference to the person in the street. Using the case stories engaged him and he could get a feeling for what was really happening with the project. Other people want statistics, so we need to collect quantitative data too."

Shankill Community Arts Network – Shaftesbury Nursery School: Artists in residence

"The evaluator used a short questionnaire with the children's parents to see what they thought their children had gained from having the artists in the nursery school. The amount of feedback from the parents really surprised me as they aren't always the best at form filling. It showed us just how much the children had gained from working with the artists and how they took some of the ideas home with them."

Inner City South Belfast Sure Start Project

"The focus groups with the parents showed us what they have gained out of Sure Start and how much their children have developed. The discussion generated some new ideas that we have been able to follow up. Another benefit was that the evaluator had done some "brief but vivids" with the Key Workers, and some of the things that came through during the focus groups supported these stories too. The evaluator held the focus groups at the crèches, which meant that she saw the children in the crèche environment, which gave her a greater insight into what we do and how we do it."

7 Making a difference

One of the main aims of the evaluation process should be to measure the impact of the project; ie. to be able to show, with supporting evidence, in which ways and for whom the project has made a difference. This can be done through using a range of evaluation approaches and tools outlined in the section above; providing both quantitative and qualitative data.

Making a difference can take various forms. At an individual level it might be that someone who has participated in new activities offered by the project has gained the confidence to enrol on a course, to enter (or return to) employment, to engage in healthy activities (eg. swimming or a keep fit class), or take up opportunities for their child to attend regularly a crèche or a pre-school scheme. For a community the project may have been the catalyst for establishing a new group to meet the interests and needs of a particular group of residents; alternatively the project may have supported the delivery of mainstream services at a local level or provided a youth worker to work with young people (that may 'keep them off the streets' thus reducing crime or the potential for crime, and/or to work with young people such that they choose to become positively involved in the community).

Take the example of running a course, and how this could make a difference. In recent years there has been a growing realisation that the 'number game' is not everything; in other words, simply recording the fact that 150 people have been on a course is relatively meaningless. This bald fact says nothing about what these 150 people have learnt, the quality of the course, the relevance of the subject matter, whether the course met expectations, or what the trainees intend to do as a result.

Evaluation of a course can take place over a number of stages:

- recording participants' expectations before they start a course;
- a mid-course review (particularly relevant if the course lasts over three days);
- a 'reactionnaire'; ie. a feedback form completed at the end of the course; sometimes called a happy sheet, as it has been proven that most people react more positively on immediate completion of a course (as they are happy to have reached the end!) than if the same questions were asked several weeks later;
- follow-up interviews, focus groups or questionnaires to see what changes (if any) have taken place as a result of the course.

If this sort of information is collected it is possible to learn something about the course content and the impact that it had on the learners. It encourages participants to reflect on the learning process and may also raise other avenues down which the project can go. At the very least if a reactionnaire is used at the end of the course five key questions can provide some insight into the course:

- In what way did the course meet your expectations?
- What did you enjoy/not enjoy about the course?
- List three things that you have learnt during the course?
- Is there anything that you want to do as a result of attending this course?
- Use three words or phrases to summarise the course overall.

A similar process can be used to evaluate any event implemented within any project – additionally asking if there is anything else that people would like to see available can also provide some ideas as to needs and interests that may support the delivery of project objectives and meeting targets.

INSPIRATIONS

Ballysillan Youth Development Project

Nine young people from Ballysillan, in North Belfast, went on a four-day residential to the North West of England. The focus of the residential was "what is community development?" At the end of the residential the young people went down to the sea, where they were set an exercise to show what they had learnt using whatever they could find on the beach. The young people not only made words out of driftwood and stones, but also drew pictures in the sand giving their impressions of what they were taking away with them from the four days. This was recorded on video, and provided a further evaluation session when they met again having returned home.

The Pathways Project – alternative education programme for fifth year pupils

"During the first year of the project we used the external evaluator to design and deliver a feedback questionnaire with the young people. Some of the feedback we got was really powerful; for example one boy wrote that "My spelling has got better and I want to read more now", and another said "Since I've been with Pathways I don't fight with Catholics in the street". In subsequent years we used the evaluation form ourselves as part of our internal evaluation and asked the evaluator to look at other aspects of the project."

© ANNA SMALLEY

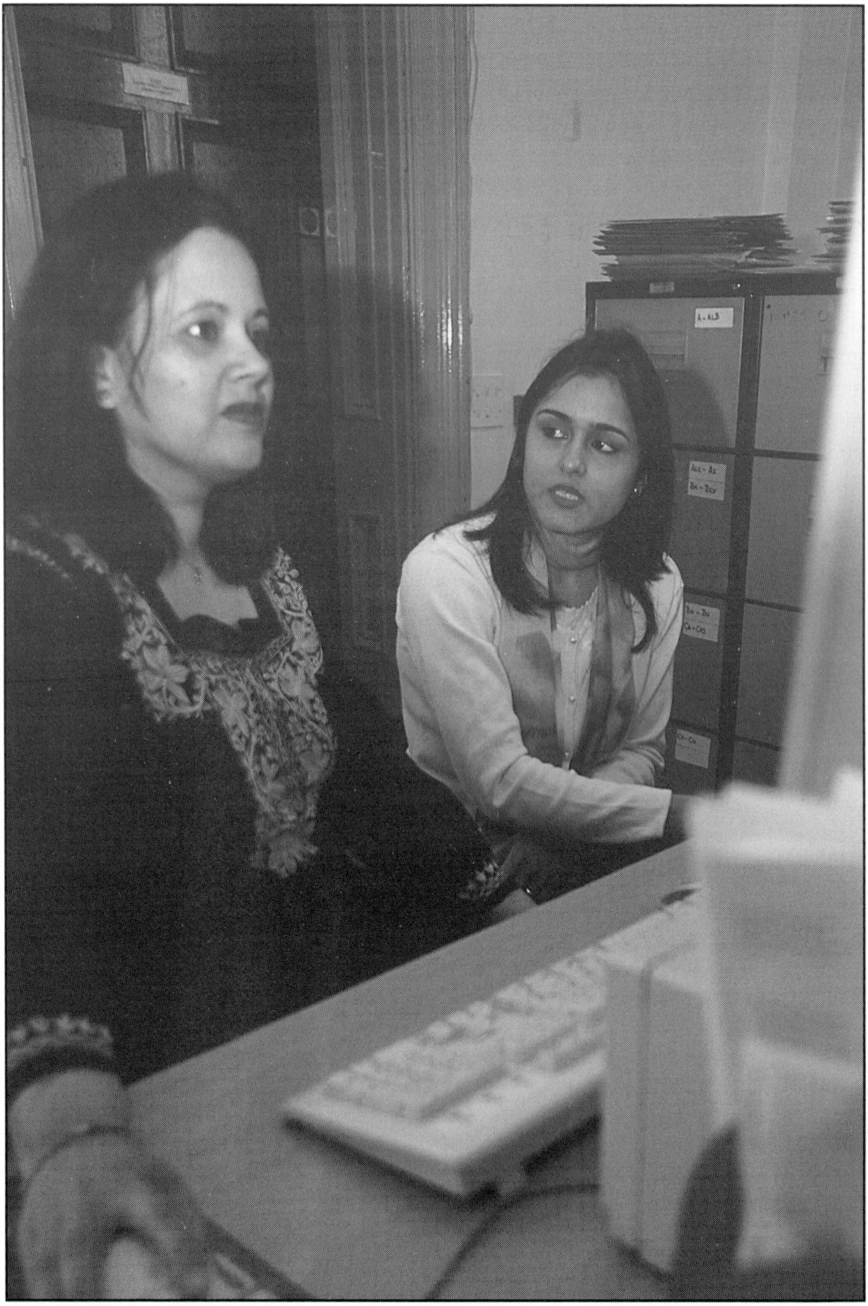

8 Qualitative indicators

Qualitative evaluation cannot be used in isolation from quantitative data, evaluation processes collecting qualitative data must be used in conjunction with other tools as qualitative data can be highly subjective. Furthermore it must be recognised that when hearing one person's opinion, be it during an interview, a focus group or when collecting case stories, this is their perception. Sometimes the evaluator strikes lucky and hears people tell the same story from different perspectives which, when looked at in the entirety, tells the same sequence of events and the same impact but from different perspectives (eg. the project worker, the beneficiary and someone from the community). Generally speaking though, evaluation can be said to be a very imprecise science.

Identifying appropriate qualitative indicators can present a problem; and having identified those aspects of community development that should be evaluated, the next question is what measurement approaches can be used.

Baseline surveys provide an initial starting point, against which progress can be measured. For some projects this can be easier than others, for example when a needs assessment or community profile may have been undertaken in the area (possibly used as evidence of need to support the project application in the first place). This can be used as a comparison when evaluating the project at different stages in time.

Statutory agencies may collect data that is made available to the project – for example, educational data or health figures. This may not always be as simple as it sounds, as all too often the way in which this data is collected is incompatible with the target area or group identified by the project.

Areas pertinent to community development in which qualitative data may be collected and impact measured include:

- social isolation;
- educational achievement;
- engaging new learners;
- employment;
- social well-being;
- healthy living;
- individual and community environment.

Some areas are easier than others; for example, within education projects it is possible to combine quantitative data (eg. qualifications attained) with qualitative data (such as personal progression, aspirations, and impact). Similarly those entering or returning to employment can be recorded both as statistical figures; but also finding out if this is the nature of work that the individual was seeking, in what way it has made a difference to their lives and the process that led them into work.

On the other hand, how to measure a reduction in social isolation or increased social well-being is more complex. To start with it is necessary to reach a common understanding on what is meant by social isolation or social well-being, which can be ascertained both through recognised definitions and that agreed by the project. It is often difficult to include the needs and challenges to those experiencing social isolation at the start of the evaluation as this socially marginalized group tend not to participate in community activities. Instead the project team should be encouraged to use systems to document individual involvement over time, recording how individuals are integrating into the community. This might be as simple as going shopping (and not just for essentials) or going for a coffee in a local café. Further steps towards social inclusion might involve joining a local group, or visiting and inviting friends to the house. Major steps towards social reintegration could involve the individual joining a community group committee, or even initiating something new within the community. The question is how to measure these changes in behaviour patterns, without making the individual feel that they are under some kind of surveillance, or increasing administrative workloads. One method could be the use of a progress framework, developed with the evaluator; where the project worker or other partners involved with the project record progress in agreement with the individual. Similar strategies can be used with awareness raising or health promotion projects, with the aim being to document where individuals were prior to involvement with the project and how they have moved on.

The Markets Health Initiative

"Twenty-five people underwent assessments with the Chest, Heart and Stroke Association. The main health problem identified was obesity. The Health Initiative started a keep fit class that begins each week with a weigh in. Over the year we will record everyone's weight loss., which will make a great press release next year – "xx pounds lost in The Markets"! There are now about 50 people coming to the class each week. As well as the fact that people are losing weight, they are also getting out and socialising, which they have said makes a difference to how they feel."

Coventry and Warwickshire Colleges: New Horizons – engaging new learners

"At the outset the Steering Group all agreed to use the same evaluation feedback form with the new learners. As a result, in excess of 1000 questionnaires were completed by new learners which gave a comprehensive picture about how the courses were received by the new learners and identified what worked most effectively for the learners in terms of promotion and content. The feedback form also gave an indication of the progression route of the new learners."

9 Building in sustainability

Evaluation can support the lobbying process seeking further funding (mainstream or additional pump-priming) for projects. However, sustainability is not simply about getting further funding. Projects can lead to change; for example, changes in service delivery by statutory agencies to better meet the needs of individuals and communities, or new or improved community resources. The evaluation process can be used to identify change and to demonstrate how the project has made a difference to the delivery of other services.

As well as demonstrating the impact on individuals and communities, the evaluation process may also address economic added value. Sometimes this is a relatively simple exercise, as it may be demonstrated that the project provides services that contribute to a more effective use of statutory resources. On other occasions the economic impact can be more difficult to demonstrate; but through research and access to relevant professional published papers it may be possible to identify ways in which the project has been cost-effective. Many projects provide intervention or prevention strategies, and while these may not have a direct economic impact in themselves, baseline data may show differences within the community that have the potential for medium- or longer-term impact.

Partnerships built during community development projects can very often be one of the most sustainable outcomes. Most projects go through both positive and negative experiences when developing working partnerships. Management committees, boards or steering groups often comprise representatives from the local community, voluntary bodies and statutory agencies; some may involve local businesses as well. The evaluation process should include the views of these stakeholders from the start, and will return to the effectiveness of the partnership both during and towards the end of the project. It is beneficial if the evaluator can tease out why the partners have chosen to commit time to the project at the outset – for some it may be because they have a financial stake in the project; for others there will be diversity in the added value gained from partnership. This may be the opportunity to network more effectively with the local community, to share and gain working knowledge, or to consider alternative ways of providing their services. It is far better to be aware of the 'agendas' of all partners at the beginning of a project; rather than for people to have hidden agendas, which may not be met, or may lead to them pushing for activities that digress from the core objectives.

As well as partners involved with the project from the outset, there may also be partnerships that develop as the project moves forward. Again, the evaluation should consider these partnerships. What are the benefits to the partners? Are there examples of good practice that may be transferable to other projects? What problems and solutions were encountered during project implementation? Have there been any changes in service delivery as a result? These issues can be addressed through a combination of questionnaires, interviews (by telephone or face-to-face) or through focus groups.

Partnerships developed initially through community development projects are often sustainable, as both the community and other agencies have experienced working relationships and entered into networks that can be called upon in the future. This can be particularly useful when partnerships have involved individuals from different sectors, eg. community, statutory, private and voluntary; who have developed contacts that they know they can work with on future occasions.

Inner City South Belfast Sure Start Project

Excerpt from the evaluation questionnaire on partnership:

Working in partnership	How this has had an impact when working with pre-school children and their families:
Improving relationships (eg. between different sectors, within communities)	
Examples of benefits to pre-school children	
Examples of benefits to families / parents	
Changes in service delivery	
Added value	

INSPIRATIONS

The Extern Organisation Time Out Project

Time Out provides a rapid response to a crisis situation that places the young person at high risk if they remain in the community. It does this by offering four days residential accommodation under full-time, one-to-one supervision. The evaluation included interviews with the Trust Gatekeepers who have an annual contract with Time Out. During the interview with one of the Gatekeepers it was identified that 75% of the young people referred by Social Workers to Time Out had not ended up in a residential children's home. He believed that without Time Out most of these young people would have been placed in residential care; and that if a young person is in care for over six weeks, statistics show that they then can remain in care for a considerable period of time. The financial outlay for Time Out is less that the cost of one week's residential care; thus, in terms of economic value it is a cost-effective programme. The Trust subsequently renewed the next year's contract.

Pathways Project – alternative education programme for fifth year pupils

"The evaluator encouraged us to network with other alternative education providers, and with her support, the Extern Organisation published a book called *Alternative Education Provision, starting to look at good practice*. We launched this at a conference in Belfast attended by about 130 people, including representatives from the Department of Education. We knew that the Department was looking at new ways to fund alternative education programmes, but the conference marked a turning point. After further consultation the Pathways project (along with other alternative education providers) now has core funding for 27 alternative education places."

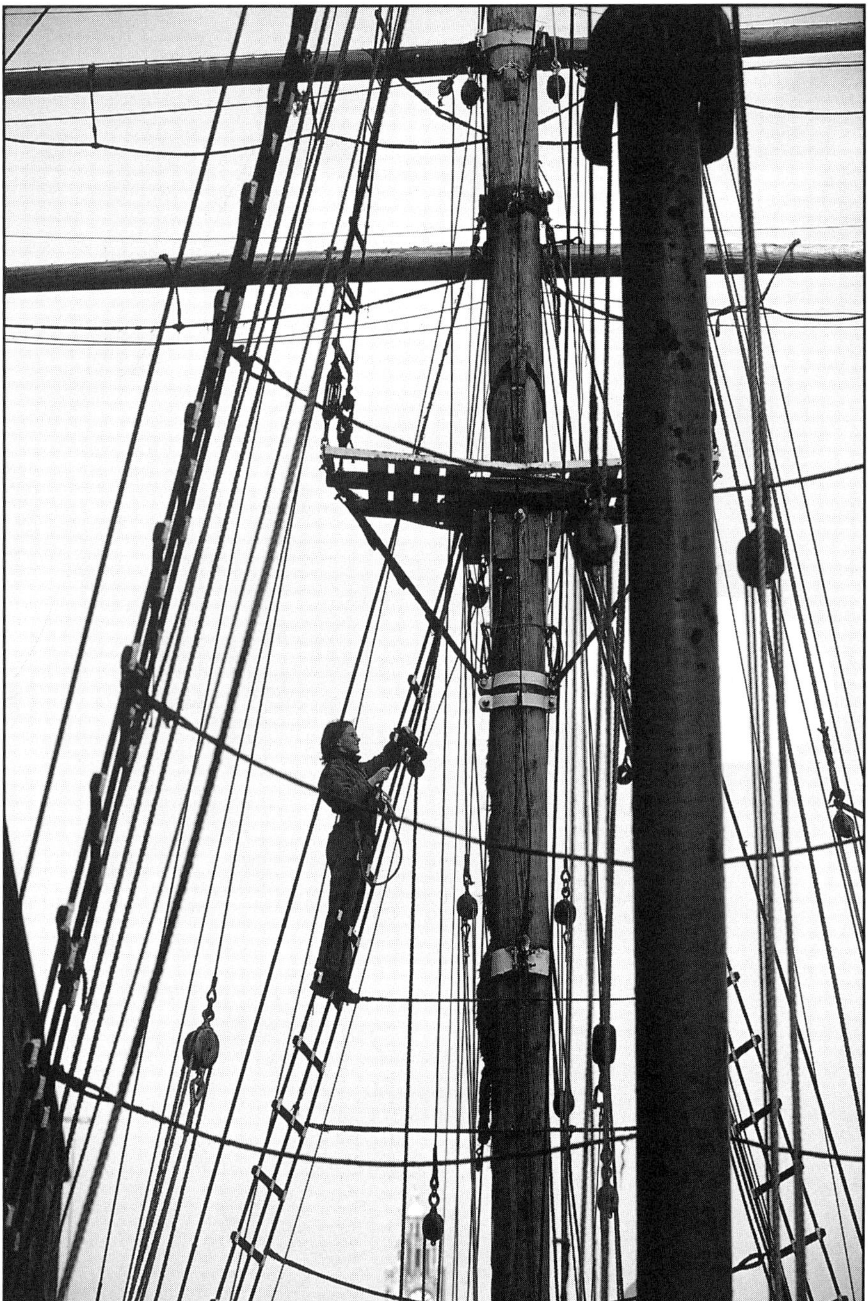

10 Spreading the word

Findings from both internal and external evaluation can be put to good use both for project promotion and dissemination activity.

Projects may choose to use quotes from the evaluation in promotional literature, particularly if this includes feedback from those living in the community; particularly effective when short excerpts from case stories are used, as a couple of 'pen pictures' can very effectively put across what the project can do.

The evaluator may be invited to contribute to presentations or other dissemination activities, such as conferences, seminars or round table discussion. Presentations can draw on the findings from the evaluation, which sometimes provides added credibility as statements are backed by evidence, and also offer the view of someone external to the project.

On other occasions, representatives from the project team or management committee use evaluation findings to support their own presentations. Having a 'bank' of overhead slides to use as appropriate saves time and can help to structure the presentation. If the evaluator has undertaken a presentation and produced either a power-point presentation or a set of overhead transparencies, they might be willing to give a copy to the project team for future use as required.

The OASIS Centre IMAGO Project – befriending those with mental ill-health difficulties

"We were fortunate enough to be allocated a slot to give a presentation up at Stormont. On this occasion we invited the evaluator to give one of the presentations about the evaluation findings, as well as involving the project team and beneficiaries. It can be much easier to have someone else demonstrating what has been achieved, rather than us just sounding self-congratulatory. The evaluator gave us a copy of the presentation, which we have since incorporated into other presentations that we have given about the project."

11 Check it out

Ten essentials to facilitate good practice when evaluating community development projects:

1. Agree why you want to evaluate the project. Who is the evaluation for? What will be done with the findings? When will the evaluation be carried out?
2. Include evaluation in the project budget.
3. Consider what can be achieved through internal monitoring and evaluation and how an external evaluator can best complement this activity.
4. Ensure that the terms of reference given to the evaluator focus on areas that will support development of the project – but at the same time maintain a degree of flexibility such that the unexpected can be included in the evaluation process.
5. Agree milestones with the evaluator, so that interim reports contribute to ongoing project reviews.
6. Start internal monitoring and data collection from the outset; quantitative data will be needed by the project team, management committees and funding bodies.
7. Link the monitoring and evaluation process to the project objectives, targets and outcomes.
8. Ensure that the evaluation has evidence to support statements and recommendations made when using both quantitative and qualitative data.
9. Community development is about collective endeavour that includes personal development and the development of communities leading to some element of change. Make certain that the evaluation process includes processes that capture qualitative data that can demonstrate the less tangible, but often key outcomes for community development projects.
10. Evaluation reports should be living documents that are exploited as a valuable resource by the project team and other stakeholders.

Glossary

Formative evaluation: an evaluation approach that contributes towards the learning, development and review process for the project. The evaluation strategy would usually be established at the outset, with evaluation activities taking place throughout the duration of the project.

Stakeholders: any individual or organisation with an interest in the project, this includes partners, management committee or board members, community groups, statutory agencies and funding bodies.

Summative evaluation: evaluation that takes place towards the end of the project.

Qualitative data: data that is concerned with quality, usually involving a number of different perspectives from a range of participants and stakeholders; can be subjective.

Quantitative data: factual data that has a numerical basis and may be used statistically (if available in sufficient quantity).

Further reading, resources and websites

Evaluation Approaches for Training and Development – A complete resource kit, Leslie Rae, Kogan Page, 1997
Materials about the validation and evaluation of training, supported by sets of resources that can be used as handouts or masters for OHP slides. Includes many checklists, ideas and systems for those involved in the process of evaluation.

PAVE (Promoting Added Value through the Evaluation of training) Evaluation Resource Pack, Jane Field, University of Plymouth, 2000
Provides a starting point in the development of evaluation tools and offers materials and information for those with responsibility to develop evaluation strategies (includes examples of evaluation tools).
Available from janefield@educationanddevelopment.co.uk

http://www.ceni.org
Community Evaluation Northern Ireland, ceni, was established in 1995 as an independent not for profit organisation to provide evaluation services to the voluntary and community sector. ceni is located within the voluntary sector with a mission to strengthen and improve the sector through a better understanding and use of evaluation.